Tammie Prince

50

Series editor
ALISTAIR
BRYCE-CLEGG

fantastic ideas for
mindfulness

FEATHERSTONE

FEATHERSTONE
Bloomsbury Publishing Plc
50 Bedford Square, London, WC1B 3DP, UK

BLOOMSBURY, FEATHERSTONE and the Feather logo are trademarks of Bloomsbury Publishing Plc

First published in Great Britain 2019 by Bloomsbury Publishing Plc

A catalogue record for this book is available from the British Library

ISBN: PB: 978-1-4729-5522-7; ePDF: 978-1-4729-5523-4

2 4 6 8 10 9 7 5 3 1

Series design: Lynda Murray

Printed and bound in India by Replika Press Pvt. Ltd.

To find out more about our authors and books visit www.bloomsbury.com and sign up for our newsletters

Contents

Introduction

Many young children do not have the skills necessary to cope with the stresses that life presents to them. They lack the tools and habits that would allow them to ride out the waves of stress as they come, and they struggle to focus on the positive aspects of life. This can have a big impact on their ability to learn. It is our moral imperative as practitioners to support the development of key strategies, such as you find in mindfulness practice, to encourage and promote good mental health now and for years to come.

Young children have a natural tendency to be mindful; they find peace and calmness in the intensity of their observations. Using mindfulness strategies from a young age allows children to develop positive habits and helps them to deal with any stresses and anxieties they may feel. Thus, mindfulness needs to become part and parcel of the daily routine of a classroom; daily deep breathing, starfish hand meditations, breathing buddies and more will help to build children's mindfulness practice and allow us to begin to change the tide towards positive mental health. Each activity in this book capitalises on the Early Years curriculum and a child's natural instincts in a positive and supportive manner.

The main aim of the book

You will find that mindfulness development isn't just about sitting still and meditating. It's about being present, enjoying moments of happiness, recognising our emotions and feelings, and learning how to bring ourselves back to a state of calm when things begin to overwhelm our minds. This book focuses activities around the breath and the use of the five senses. The ideas set up opportunities for children to develop kindness towards others and gratitude for what they have in their life. Could there be a better gift to give a child?

The main aim of this book is to give Early Years practitioners quick and easy activities that build on the natural mindfulness young children have. The foundation of good practice is to integrate mindfulness into the everyday practice of the classroom. The activities enable you to develop positive mental health skills of all children in the group and support mindfulness practice outside the classroom and into home life too.

Looking after your own mental health

What is the key to successfully integrating mindfulness practice in the classroom? YOUR mindfulness development! We must not forget about or neglect our own positive mental health. If you work on your own mindfulness, you will accelerate the development of the practice in your children. It is essential that the adults become good role models for the children. By developing your own practice, you become a more mindful teacher – calmer, more reflective, more focused in the moment and better able to rejoice in the positives of daily school life. Children will feel and feed off this energy.

Not all of the activities in this book will be successful with all children and you, as a practitioner, may not be comfortable with some of the ideas. Begin by picking and choosing the ones you feel most comfortable with and then move on to those that may challenge you or your children more. Now it is time to dive in. Inhale… exhale… and begin!

The structure of the book

Before you start any activity, read through everything on the page so you are familiar with the whole activity and what you might need to plan in advance. The pages are all organised in the same way.

What you need lists the resources required for the activity. These are likely to be readily available in most settings or can be bought or made easily.

What to do tells you step-by-step what you need to do to complete the activity.

The **Health & Safety tips** are often obvious, but safety can't be overstressed. In many cases there are no specific hazards involved in completing the activity, and your usual health and safety measures should be enough. In others there are particular issues to be noted and addressed.

Taking it forward gives ideas for additional activities on the same theme, or for developing the activity further. These will be particularly useful for things that have gone especially well or where children show a real interest. In many cases they use the same resources, and in every case they have been designed to extend learning and broaden the children's experiences.

Finally, **What's in it for the children?** tells you (and others) briefly how the suggested activities contribute to learning.

Just breathe

Basic, fun breathing exercises

What you need:

- Nothing

Top tip ⭐

Breathing is an easy strategy to incorporate into your teaching as it can happen at any time and in any place, e.g. at the beginning of each lesson, during transition times or any time the children seem restless.

What's in it for the children?

Mindful breathing exercises change energy from tension to relaxation. It does this by turning off the part of the brain that produces stress hormones. It helps children to calm down.

Taking it forward

- Have the children teach their favourite breathing strategy to their parents, another class or to the whole school during a whole-school assembly. When children become role models, they are developing their emotional intelligence and learning to support others.

- Teach children to choose a breathing technique and use it immediately when they feel upset or angry.

What to do:

Belly breathing

1. Ask the children to place their hands on their bellies, then take a deep breath in for four counts, blowing their belly up like a balloon.

2. Ask them to hold the breath for one count and then slowly exhale for six counts, deflating the balloon in their belly.

Snake breathing

1. Ask the children to sit up tall and take a deep breath in, filling up their whole body.

2. Have them pause and exhale slowly and smoothly, making a hissing sound for as long as they can as they exhale.

Birthday candle breathing

1. Describe a wonderful birthday cake with all its bright candles to the group. Ask them to inhale deeply as you do.

2. Invite them to blow out the candles by exhaling strongly through the mouth.

3. Pretend that the candles have not all been blown out and have them repeat the process as many times as needed.

Elephant breathing

1. Encourage children to choose something to shower themselves with, e.g. love, laughter or strength.

2. Ask them to stand with their feet wide apart, link their hands and dangle their arms in front of them like an elephant trunk.

3. Get them to inhale through their nose as they raise their arms high above their head and lean back while thinking about the emotion they have chosen.

4. Invite them to exhale through their mouth as they swing their arms down through their legs.

Dragon's breath

A fun deep-breathing activity

What you need:

- Cardboard tube
- Scissors
- Sticky tape
- Markers, crayons, paint, stickers and other bright and shiny bits and pieces to decorate the tube
- Thin, light streamers and ribbon

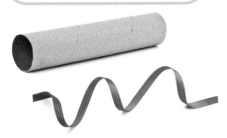

What to do:

1. Cut about 1 cm off the top of the cardboard tube so you have a ring. Put this aside as you will need it later.
2. Cut a straight line up through the remainder of the tube.
3. Squeeze the tube to make a thinner tube and secure it with sticky tape on the top and bottom.
4. Invite the children to decorate the tube. This will be the handle.
5. Tape thin streamers and ribbon around the inside edge of the smaller ring that was cut off the tube in step 1.
6. Tape the smaller ring to the end of the decorated tube so it looks like a bubble wand.
7. Now it's time to make dragon's breath. Take a deep belly breath and blow through the ring, making the streamers wave and flap like fire from a dragon.
8. Invite the children to take turns making dragon's breath.

> ## Top tip ⭐
> Remind children to focus on the breath, how it flows from their lungs, noses and mouths and how it makes their bodies feel.

What's in it for the children?

The dragon's breath wand makes deep breathing fun for young children which is important. The key is getting them to take deep breaths in and blow all the air out of their lungs to make their natural calming reflexes kick in.

Taking it forward

- Ignite the children's imaginations in an outdoor area by pairing up half the children with dragon's breath wands and the other half with bubble wands and solution. Children can fight the dragons by blowing bubbles – lots of deep breathing all round!

Flower breathing
Reinforcing the rhythm of breathing

What you need:

- A large five-petal flower template, one per child
- Crayons
- Felt tip markers
- Coloured pencils

Top tip ⭐

When the children have decorated their flower for the first time, discuss how they can use it to focus them when they are upset, anxious, angry, etc.

What's in it for the children?

Each day we take over 20,000 breaths. This automatic bodily function keeps us alive and helps to regulate our emotions. When we bring attention to our breathing, we take control of our emotions and reactions through mindful purpose.

Taking it forward

- Place the flowers around the room and use them as part of your transition time, e.g. at the beginning of the day, before lunch, after lunch, before they go home.

What to do:

1. Choose a mindful theme and have children decorate their own five-petal flower for meditation. Themes they could consider include:

   a. Gratitude – each petal depicts a different thing or person the child is grateful for in their lives.

   b. Positive thoughts – each petal depicts something that makes them happy.

   c. Kindness – each petal depicts a way they can be kind to themselves and others.

2. Once complete, have each child place it near where they work, in their favourite area of provision or in the mindfulness corner (see p. 60).

3. When the child is feeling anxious, invite the child to:

   a. Trace a petal and inhale. They should hold their breath at the point, exhale and focuses on the picture in that petal as they trace the other side of the petal.

   b. They should keep going until they've traced around the whole flower.

   c. Then they should touch the centre of the flower, taking a deep breath (see p. 6) and close their eyes for a moment.

   d. Repeat as necessary.

Smell the roses

An imaginative mindful breathing exercise

What you need:

- Red tissue paper
- Green card or construction paper
- Scissors
- Pipe cleaners
- Aroma scents (a list can be found on p. 44)

Top tip ⭐

For greatest impact, create a selection of flowers all with different scents so that children are able to choose the one that they enjoy the most.

What's in it for the children?

The more they practise mindful breathing, the more it becomes part of a positive habit that children will access automatically when anxious, upset, mad, etc.

Taking it forward

- Get the children to make a bouquet of flowers to take home and encourage the family to take part in mindful deep breathing as a way to start or end the day at home.

Preparation:

1. Cut tissue paper into six to ten equal rectangles.
2. Lay each piece on top of each other.
3. Fold in accordion style.
4. Loop a pipe cleaner tightly around the middle of the folded tissue paper strip.
5. Gently separate the tissue paper sheets, pulling them towards the centre, to unfold the petals of your flower. Fluff to shape the flower.
6. Cut leaves out of the green card and glue them to the pipe cleaner.
7. Put a few drops of aroma scents on the centre sheets of the flowers.

What to do:

8. Use the flowers as part of a breathing meditation with the children.
9. Encourage them to sit up tall and hold their flower by the stem. Look at the petals, their shape and colour.
10. Invite them to bring the flower up to their nose and take a deep belly breath, then remove the flower and breath out. Repeat for around 15 breaths.
11. Ask the children how the scent makes them feel. Does it make them think about anything or recall any memories?

Play dough meditation

Using the senses in active meditation

What you need:

- Meditation music
- One small ball of play dough per child

Top tip ⭐

Don't be discouraged if the children want to be very verbal the first few times they do this mediation. Gently remind them to answer the questions in their head and focus only on the play dough. On repeated meditations you will find the children become quieter and more focused. Mindfulness takes practise.

What to do:

1. Set the scene by having all the children find a comfortable sitting position and put on some calming meditation music.

2. Give each child a small ball of the play dough and instruct them NOT to play with it, roll it or squish it.

3. Invite the children to take three deep belly breaths (see p. 6).

4. Instruct them to look at the play dough. Discuss the urge to squeeze it. Ask the children questions to provoke their responses, such as 'Is the play dough hot, warm or cold?', 'How would you describe the colour of the play dough?'.

5. Encourage the children to move it from hand to hand. Does the shape change?

6. Invite them to sniff the play dough and notice the smell of it.

7. Let the children push a finger into the play dough. Can they see their fingerprint? What does it look like?

8. Then instruct the children to continue to squeeze, roll and make the dough into shapes. Remind them to concentrate only on the play dough, how it feels in their hands and the smell of dough.

9. Complete the meditation by having the children take three deep, belly breaths.

50 fantastic ideas for mindfulness

What's in it for the children?

The use of observation with the senses allows children to focus in the moment, allowing the natural therapeutic qualities of play dough to encourage calmness and relaxation.

Taking it forward

- Make your own play dough and add natural scents, e.g. cinnamon, nutmeg, allspice or vanilla. The scents will enhance the sensory aspect of the meditation and help to set positive, happy memories around the scent.

- Allow children to choose their favourite colour and scent of play dough. Put it in a resealable bag or container to keep in a special place and use when they feel anxious.

Starfish hand meditation
Divert and refocus the mind

What you need:

- Meditation music
- Two hands

What to do:

1. Set the scene by having all the children find a comfortable sitting position and put on some calming meditation music.

2. Ask the children to close their eyes, breathe deeply and spread their fingers out like a starfish on one hand.

3. Ask them to use the pointing finger on the other hand to trace around their outstretched fingers. Instruct children to inhale as they trace up each finger and exhale when they move down.

4. Encourage them to concentrate only on how it feels and let other thoughts float away.

5. Continue until the children are relaxed and calm.

Top tip

Don't get too caught up in a right or wrong way of doing the meditation. Focus on how it makes them feel. They are beginning to learn that mediations are personal to them, and they need to discover what works for them.

What's in it for the children?

Children gain an independent mindfulness strategy that gives them control of their emotions in a tactile and focused manner.

Taking it forward

- After you have shown and practised this strategy with the children several times, encourage them to do it independently whenever they are feeling anxious, upset, cross, etc.

Leaf meditation
Appreciate the natural world

What you need:

- At least one leaf per child
- A quiet space

What to do:

1. Ask the children to cup their hands in front of them. Lay one leaf in the hands of every child.

2. Invite them to notice the colours in their leaf, the different shades of colours and the fading of one colour into another.

3. Encourage them to notice the veins in the leaf, the main stem and the edges of the leaf.

4. Suggest that they feel the leaf by running their fingers over the top and bottom, and along the edges, noticing the differences. They could rub it against their face or over the top of their hand to use nerve endings that normally are not used to feel objects.

5. Now invite them to smell the leaf and pay attention to the scent. They should inhale deeply and notice the memories it may bring up.

6. Have them close their eyes and take a minute to breathe deeply and allow themselves to be in awe and wonder of the moment they have had with the leaf before they return to their play.

What's in it for the children?

In this activity the children practise the important mindfulness strategy of observation and appreciation of the world around them in a way that can bring immediate peacefulness.

Taking it forward

- Use other natural objects as catalysts for meditation, e.g. flowers, snow, fruits, vegetables, pieces of wood, pebbles, fabrics.

- Use this mindful observation to start a new topic as it provides a powerful sensory experience to hook the new learning experiences together.

✚ Health & Safety

If collecting leaves with the children, ensure that the area is free from any dangerous debris, nettles or biting insects.

Storytime meditation

Turn storytime into a calm meditation

What you need:

- A storybook of around five minutes on a topic that supports mindfulness development, e.g. kindness, love, friendship, perseverance

What to do:

1. Before you begin, have the children get comfortable either lying down or sitting up.

2. Instruct them to take deep belly breaths (see p. 6).

3. Ask them to close their eyes and listen to you reading the story.

4. In a soft voice, read the story. Do not comment or ask questions during the story as you read. If the children seem to be getting wiggly, talk them through a couple of deep belly breaths.

5. When the story is complete, guide them through a couple of deep belly breaths then ask them to open their eyes and give their body a big stretch.

6. Discuss the story. How did it make them feel? What did they learn from the story? How was the experience different to your usual storytime?

Top tip ⭐

Some children will find it difficult to close their eyes for a variety of reasons. Remind them that is OK and if they can't close their eyes, they can look at a small spot on the floor as you read the story.

What's in it for the children?

By closing their eyes and performing deep belly breaths, children are allowed to focus entirely on the story. This gives them time to relax and develop positive attitudes to the life situations represented in the story.

Taking it forward

- If successful, try social stories that you create yourself based on something that has happened in the class or the needs of the group. This is good to use for learning the rules of the class and society and how to deal with things that don't go their way.

Colour meditation
Active observation meditation

What you need:

- Objects in the chosen colour
- A bell

Top tip ⭐

When you do this meditation for the first time, take a few minutes to practise using the signal and talking them through the belly breathing, noticing the object and then taking another belly breath.

What's in it for the children?

The children get practice in observation skills, identification of colours and providing moments of calm reflection to support their mindfulness development.

Taking it forward

- Once children have done this meditation a few times, instead of choosing a colour for the day, at the signal tell the children which colour they are to observe. With each signal, change the colour choice.

- Choose a variety of times during the day to use the 'Colour meditation' including transition times.

What to do:

1. At the beginning of the day, introduce the colour. Take a minute to have the children notice the objects and people wearing that colour. Ask them the question, 'How does the colour make you feel?' and give them time to discuss.

2. Explain that when they hear the bell or other signal, they are to take a deep belly breath and while they are looking for something that colour, they should take another deep belly breath.

3. Periodically, throughout the day, give the signal. At the end of the day, guide the children by asking them questions:

   - Have you noticed something or someone you have never noticed before?

   - How many different things did you notice or did you keep noticing the same thing?

Pebble meditation
Developing gratitude and kindness

What you need:

- Two pebbles each

Top tip ⭐

Allow the children to decorate their pebbles with paints to personalise them.

What's in it for the children?

Children can begin to develop social and emotional skills by focusing on gratitude, kindness and empathy. The purpose of this activity is to connect the idea of doing something for someone else with positive emotions.

Taking it forward

- Once the practice is established, introduce a mantra for the children to whisper as they squeeze each pebble, e.g. 'I am happy and thankful' or 'I am kind and thoughtful'.

What to do:

1. Ask the children to decide on something or someone that makes them happy, then ask them to think about something they could do to make someone else happy.

2. Ask them to sit up straight and relax, placing one pebble in each hand.

3. Guide the children to close their eyes, squeeze the first pebble and think about the thing that makes them happy. Have them focus on the thought and the feel of the pebble in their hand. Then get them to relax their hand.

4. Ask the children to squeeze the other pebble and think about one thing they could do to make someone else happy. Have them focus on the thought and the feel of the pebble in their hand. Then get them to relax their hand.

5. Repeat the cycle three times, reminding the children to take deep belly breaths.

Superhero mindfulness

Using body language to boost confidence and reduce anxiety

What you need:

- Meditation music

What to do:

1. Play meditation music softly in the background.

2. Discuss superhero poses that the children might have seen in films and on television. Invite each child to choose a pose that makes them feel good and strong.

3. Tell the children that they are to close their eyes and get into their superhero pose.

4. Have children focus on their deep belly breathing as they pretend to be a superhero.

5. After approximately two minutes, have the children open their eyes, stretch and relax.

6. Discuss how they feel and what they were thinking of when they were pretending to be superheroes.

Top tip ⭐

The first time you do this activity, explain to the children that they will become superheroes. Discuss how superheroes stand, with their arms spread out, legs spread and head held high. Identify how this makes superheroes feel – powerful, confident, calm. Practise the pose a few times so they understand the pose and can look at others as they pose.

What's in it for the children?

The body language of the 'Superhero mindfulness' activity reduces anxiety, improves children's ability to deal with stress and boosts their confidence.

Taking it forward

- Practise some scenarios where the children may be scared to do something or are in situations that make them upset. Discuss how they can use their Superhero mindfulness pose to help them feel better.

Breathing buddies

A focused breathing strategy for school and home

What you need:

- Soft, calm meditation music (optional)

- A stuffed animal, one each

Top tip ⭐

Combine this strategy with Snake bags (see p. 50).

What to do:

1. Turn down the lights and have children lie on the floor with their stuffed animal and get comfortable. Turn on the meditation music.

2. Instruct the children to close their eyes to begin.

3. Ask them to place their stuffed animal on their belly and take a deep breath in for four counts, blowing their belly up like a balloon so the stuffed animal rises.

4. They should hold their breath for one count and then slowly exhale for six counts, deflating the balloon in their belly so the stuffed animal falls.

5. Encourage the children to reflect on the experience. Can they feel their animal rise with their belly as they inhale? How does it feel? Do they feel the pressure of the toy on their belly?

6. Continue to talk them through a few more breaths and then explain they will now do this on their own. Remind them one more time how it is done, then monitor the children as they breathe independently.

What's in it for the children?

The comforting touch of stuffed animal allows children to focus on their breathing. Breathing deeply reduces the levels of stress hormones in the body and increases the relaxation chemicals that will support their positive mental health and wellbeing.

Taking it forward

- Encourage children to use this strategy at home, particularly at night when they go to bed.

- Ensure that you explain the strategy to parents so they can encourage this calming, sleep-inducing strategy.

- Personalise this strategy by having children bring their own stuffed animals from home.

Mandala magic
Make and use a mandala

What you need:

- Templates of mandalas
- Rolling pins, one per child
- A ball of play dough, one per child
- Baking paper
- A selection of seeds, beans, flowers and shells
- PVC glue

What to do:

1. Place a selection of mandala templates around the work area for inspiration.
2. Ask the children to roll out the ball of play dough so that it makes a circle on a piece of baking paper.
3. Using the selection of seeds, beans, flowers and shells, invite the children to create a design by pushing the items into the dough.
4. When finished, allow the mandalas to air dry for three to four days.
5. Once the mandala is dry, cover it in PVC glue to seal.

What's in it for the children?

The creation of mandalas and the mandala meditation can help children to explore their feelings without using words but by using colour and design. The children can then use mandalas to assist in focusing attention through observation, while also relieving stress and anxiety.

Taking it forward

- Use the mandalas as part of a meditation. Play calming music and encourage the children to focus on the centre of their mandala design while doing some mindful breathing. Let them know it is OK for their gaze to wander to other parts of the mandala; they should notice the designs, colours and ways the lines meet each other.

- Use the mandalas as part of a meditation. Play calming music and encourage the children to focus n the centre of their mandala design while doing some mindful breathing (see p. 6).

Health & Safety

Note any children that have specific allergies and use alternatives such as clay instead of dough and beads instead of seeds to create mandalas.

Top tip

Younger children may not fully grasp the circular patterns of mandalas and the designs may be more chaotic. That is fine – the designs belong to them.

Squish and relax
Beginning muscle relaxation meditation

What you need:

- A small ball of play dough per child
- Meditation music (optional)

What to do:

1. Have the children sit comfortably with the ball of play dough in one hand. Play soft, gentle music in the background if you like.

2. Ask them take a deep breath. In a gentle voice, guide them to breathe in for five counts, hold for one count and exhale for eight counts.

3. Direct them to become aware of their body and instruct them to slowly move their awareness to the dough, noticing the sensations from their arms and hands.

4. Tell them to squeeze the ball tightly like they are trying to pick up a heavy weight. Have them hold this pose for a count of five, then relax.

5. Repeat this cycle over a period of a minute.

6. Have the children remain at rest for a few more deep breaths, being aware of their breathing.

7. Repeat with the other hand.

8. Discuss with the children how their bodies felt during and after the activity. What did they notice? How could this help them when they are angry, upset or anxious?

Top tip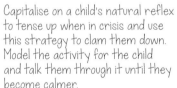

Capitalise on a child's natural reflex to tense up when in crisis and use this strategy to clam them down. Model the activity for the child and talk them through it until they become calmer.

What's in it for the children?

This muscle relaxation method addresses a child's natural tendency to tense up in a crisis. The exercise helps children to lower their overall stress levels and relax.

Taking it forward

- Encourage the use of the 'Squish and relax' routine without play dough and use it as part of a more advanced body scan meditation that includes the whole body.

Stone stacking

Enhancing simple focus

What you need:

- A collection of stones of different sizes, each no larger than the palm of your hand
- A few photographs of stone towers so that children get the idea of the task.
- A quiet place to do the stacking
- Camera or sketch pad (optional)

What to do:

1. Allow the children to explore the stones. Ask them questions such as, 'How does it feel?', 'Is it heavy or light?' and 'Is it smooth or rough?'.
2. Model how to stack the stones into towers and show the children photographs of stacked stones as evidence that it can be done.
3. Discuss the need to balance the stones and how they need to be calm to balance the stones just right.
4. Then set a challenge, e.g. 'How many stones can you use to make a tower?'.
5. Children can take a photograph or sketch their finished stone tower.

Top tip ⭐

Ensure the stones have some flatness on one side to allow them to stack easily.

What's in it for the children?

Stone stacking is a mini-meditation. It gives children the opportunity to be quiet, think and focus just on what they are doing. Their silent, fixed attention is fully in the moment as they balance the stones.

Taking it forward

- Use stone stacking as part of a zen garden (see p. 28) in the classroom or a stone garden in the outdoor provision.
- Invite children and families to contribute to the collection of stones.
- Encourage families to take photographs of any stone stacks that they make on their own adventures and include them in a classroom display.

Magnetic hands

Focusing on the present moment

What you need:

- Nothing

What to do:

1. Ask the children to stand with their hands shoulder width apart with palms facing outwards and facing a partner.

2. Encourage them to take a deep belly breath and exhale very slowly.

3. Ask them to pretend there are magnets in their hands. Ask the children to inhale as you count slowly to four. The children should slowly bring their hands close together until they almost touch.

4. Instruct the children to exhale to the count of four as they move their hands back to where they began.

Top tip ⭐

If the children insist on pushing their hands together, this is OK. It will support those children that need sensory pressure to help them relax and become calm.

What's in it for the children?

This strategy gives children a visual focal point for practising deep mindful breathing and supports training the mind to purposefully focus attention on the present moment.

Taking it forward

- Encourage children to take ownership of mindfulness practice and have them lead each other in this strategy. Put photographs of the children using the strategy in the mindfulness corner (see p. 60) to encourage its use.

Labyrinths

Focused attention that brings peace and calmness

What you need:

- A printed finger labyrinth for each child

Top tip

Search online for 'free printable finger labyrinths'. There are a number of good, free labyrinths available.

What to do:

1. Children should sit comfortably with the labyrinth in front of them and take deep breaths as they focus on it.

2. Invite them to place their pointer finger on it and slowly trace the pattern. You should continue to encourage deep belly breathing.

3. Children should stop momentarily at the centre of the labyrinth, take a deep breath and then retrace their path out of the labyrinth. As each child will reach the centre in their own time, you should model how to do this.

4. Once the children get the idea of how to trace the path with their dominant hand, have them switch to their non-dominant hand. This will force deeper focus and concentration.

What's in it for the children?

This strategy allows children to be focused on the present with deep breathing that relaxes and calms the body and allows them to enjoy the present moment.

Taking it forward

- Print out a number of labyrinth photos and encourage children to create their own outdoor labyrinths using play equipment, leaves, branches, sticks, etc.

Worry stones

A self-soothing mindfulness strategy

What you need:

- Small ball of play dough per child (see recipe below)
- PVC glue
- Ingredients for dough:
  - 260 g flour
  - 130 g salt
  - 235 ml water
  - Food colouring or spices (optional)
- Oven (optional)

Top tip

Ensure that the worry stones are easily accessible so that the children can use them when they need them and not just during whole-group meditation sessions. This will support their independent mindfulness development.

What's in it for the children?

The gentle rhythm of rubbing of the stone and breathing deeply allows the mind to relax and reduces anxiety. It allows for independent self-soothing which is an important life skill.

Taking it forward

- Encourage children to independently use the worry stones and breathing when they are feeling upset, angry, sad, etc.
- Combine this activity with the Play dough meditation (see p. 10).

What to do:

1. Make the dough by combining the ingredients in a bowl. If the dough is too dry, add a few drops of water. If the dough is too wet, add a little bit of flour.
2. Divide the dough and give each child a small ball.
3. Ask them to slightly flatten the ball into the palm of their hand and place it on the table.
4. Ask them to softly press their thumb into the centre, leaving a small well.
5. With damp fingertips, they should softly smooth the edges and cracks.
6. Air dry the stones for three days or oven dry for 20 minutes at 200°C.
7. Coat the stones with a thin layer of PVC glue. Allow it to dry and coat them once more. This will seal them and give a smooth surface to the worry stones.
8. When dried, have the children use their stones in a simple breathing meditation. Have them hold the stone between the index finger and thumb and gently move their thumb back and forth across the stone. While doing this, they should take deep, slow belly breaths (see p. 6), focusing on the feel of the stone in their hand and the feel of the air as they inhale and exhale.

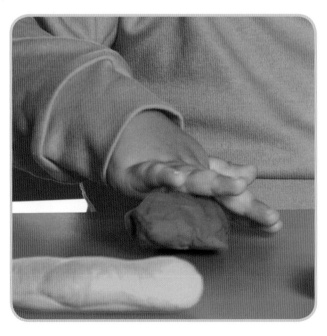

Chopstick challenge

Advanced mindful concentration

What you need:

- Child-friendly chopsticks
- Small, light building blocks
- A quiet place to do the stacking
- Camera

Top tip ⭐

Remind children to practise active, slow, deep breathing when they are stacking.

What's in it for the children?

This activity is a bit more advanced and requires greater concentration and skill than stone stacking as children have to focus not only on balancing the objects to build a tower but also to manipulate the chopsticks. In addition to developing their ability to 'be in the moment', it also supports fine motor development.

Taking it forward

- Remove the 'training wheels' of child-friendly chopsticks. Swap them for regular chopsticks that require even greater concentration and fine motor control.
- To keep calm, remind the children that if the tower falls, they can simply close their eyes, take three mindful breaths and start again.

What to do:

1. Allow the children to explore the feel of the chopsticks and how they work.
2. Model how to stack the blocks into towers using the chopsticks to pick them up and put them in position.
3. Discuss how the children need to be calm to balance the blocks just right and how they need to concentrate to use the chopsticks.
4. Challenge the children to build a tower using a certain number of blocks. Decide on the number of blocks for each child so they can easily complete the task and feel successful.
5. Invite them to take a photograph of their finished block tower.

Zen garden
A calming small world activity

What you need:

- Dry sand
- Shallow tray
- Natural objects, e.g. polished rocks, seashells, tree bark, small twigs
- Craft sticks

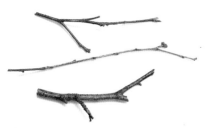

What to do:

1. Pour dry sand in a shallow tray and place the natural items around the edge.

2. Using the craft sticks, have the children smooth out the sand.

3. Invite the children to make tracks in the sand with their fingers and the twigs.

4. Have them arrange the natural objects in a pleasing pattern or design. They can trace paths around the shells and stones with their twigs. Try to ensure that the environment is quiet and relaxed so the children can focus solely on the activity.

5. Once complete, have the children do a simple one-minute breathing meditation as they focus on the sand, lines and objects.

Top tip ⭐

Take photographs of the completed zen gardens children created to use in the mindfulness corner (see p. 60).

What's in it for the children?

A 'Zen garden' for children gives a small world focus that allows children to explore natural materials through calm, relaxing play. When the garden is completed, it adds continued value by providing a focus for meditation exercises.

Taking it forward

- Have children create larger Zen gardens in outdoor areas of the provision such as in sand pits or beach play areas. The objects need to be equally large in size to balance the design, e.g. larger stones, branches, leaves. Use larger dowel rods, racks and shovels to create the track lines.

Mindful treasure hunt

Encourage children to explore the environment

What you need:

- One basket per pair
- A clipboard per pair
- A checklist with icons or pictures to indicate sight, smell, hearing, taste and touch

What to do:

1. Discuss the five different senses with the children and how they are like superpowers.

2. Explain to the children that they will be going on a special treasure hunt and they will be using their very special powers (senses) to find the treasures. Ask them to get into pairs.

3. Go through the checklist and discuss what objects might fit into each category, e.g. a flower could be a 'smell'. This will help them to know what they are looking for in the environment around them.

4. Set a timer and then send them out on their treasure hunt to experience the different objects on the checklist.

5. Once the time is up, bring the children back together and have them share their treasures with everyone.

Top tip ⭐

For the first time or with your youngest children, you may choose to focus on one sense at a time and discuss what that sense means. Have the children go out and hunt for it and return to the group once they have found a relevant item.

What's in it for the children?

This activity encourages children to notice the environment around them and appreciate the senses they use to explore that environment.

Taking it forward

- Set up a treasure hunt station in an area of provision and have the children focus on one sense per day. They can add their treasure hunt finds to this area to explore as a group at the end of the day.

Mindful paint doodling

A strategy that allows children to enjoy being in the moment

What you need:

- Liquid paints
- Large clear plastic bags
- Sticky tape
- Cotton buds

Top tip

Tape the bags securely to a window to give the activity a different perspective. Encourage the children to focus on the sunlight as it shines through the paints and the bag.

What to do:

1. Add a few squirts of paint into a large sealable plastic bag. Secure the opening with sticky tape.

2. Tape the paint-filled bag onto a flat surface.

3. Encourage the children to use the cotton buds like a pencil and draw lines, squiggles, curves and curls in the paint. Remind children to focus on their breathing and pay attention to how the cotton bud feels as they create the lines.

4. To repeat, have the child smooth out the paint in the bag and begin again.

What's in it for the children?

This activity requires the children to slow down – focusing on the paint bag and cotton bud and doodling repeatedly with full attention. It also helps develop their fine motor skills.

Taking it forward

- Place this activity in the mindfulness corner (see p. 60) and encourage its use when children need some extra calm time.

- Have children try doodling on small sheets of paper with coloured crayons, pencils or felt tips. Always encourage the children to focus on their breathing, the feel of the movement when making the lines and look of the doodles against the paper.

Mindful table colouring
Mindful colouring on a large scale

What you need:

- A mandala template
- A printer and printer paper
- An assortment of crayons, pencils, felt tips and markers
- Soft mediation music (optional)

What to do:

1. Enlarge the mandala template so that it would be big enough to cover a table and then print it out. You may need to print several A4 sheets and stick them together. Alternatively, if you are good at drawing, cover the table in a large sheet of paper and draw one large mandala.

2. Discuss with the children the importance of cooperation and how we can support one another in mindful ways.

3. In small groups, allow children to colour the large mandala using the art materials.

4. Encourage the children to focus on the designs and only colour in small areas at a time.

Top tip ⭐

Make sure you position sticky tape at the back of the mandalas. You will want the children to be able to colour all areas.

What's in it for the children?

Collaborative mindful colouring encourages cooperation which develops relationships and a calm environment. Children need to negotiate space and be respectful of others' intentions.

Taking it forward

- Divide a large sheet of paper into 5 cm squares. Then encourage children to draw and colour their own small mandala in each square to make a patchwork of mandalas.

Mindful hand massage
A mindful self-soothing option

What you need:
- Soft, calm meditation music
- Hand lotion

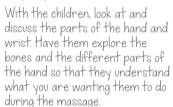

Top tip ⭐

With the children, look at and discuss the parts of the hand and wrist. Have them explore the bones and the different parts of the hand so that they understand what you are wanting them to do during the massage.

What's in it for the children?

Mindful hand massages allow children to relax their muscles, calm their breathing and improve their mood. It reduces pain, stress, anxiety and tension by way of a natural reflex.

Taking it forward

- During the massage, continue to remind the children that all the motions need to be soft, with focus being on their breathing and the sensations they are feeling when they are massaging their hands.

Health & Safety
Be aware of all allergies and check that the hand lotion you are using is safe for your children.

What to do:

1. Set the mood by lowering the brightness of the lights of the classroom and putting on some meditation music.

2. Ask the children to sit up straight and take three deep belly breaths and clear their minds. They should put their hands out in front of them.

3. Put a small squirt of hand lotion in the children's hands. Encourage them to rub the lotion over the entire hand and wrist area in slow, gentle strokes.

4. Model and guide the children to use the thumb to rub small, gentle circles around the opposite hand, then use the thumb to continue to rub in small circles between bones on the top of the hand.

5. Follow the natural lines along the hand towards the fingers. Take each finger in turn and use the thumb to rub in the same circular motion along each finger from base to fingertip.

6. Pull each finger softly by the fingertip. Clasp hands together, entwining the fingers (like in prayer) and move hands and wrists back and forth, left to right and in soft circular motions.

7. Turn the hand over and use the same small, gentle circular motions of the thumb to rub the palm of the hand starting at the thumb base and then working your way up the palm to the top near the fingers.

8. Repeat steps 5 to 7 on other hand.

9. Complete the massage by repeating step 3. Invite the children to lay their hands in their laps and take three more deep breaths.

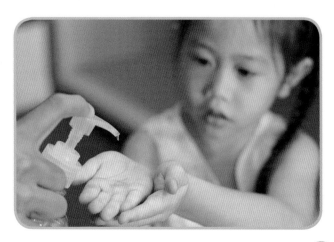

Cat's whiskers massage

A simple, calming facial massage

What you need:

- Hand-washing facilities
- Soft, calm meditation music

Top tip ⭐

Model the way you should hold your fingers and the amount of pressure you use. Have the children practise outside the meditation before using it as part of the meditation.

What's in it for the children?

Massage and the power of touch reduces stress hormones. The lowering of stress hormones not only reduces the feelings of anxiety but also supports a healthier immune system.

Taking it forward

- If successful, try an ear massage. Use your entire hand and cup the top of each of your ears and gently squeeze for a count of five. Move down the ears, continuing to gently squeeze for a count of five. Finish by placing your thumbs in the dent behind the bottom of your ear lobe (where it joins your face) and apply gentle pressure for a count of five.

What to do:

1. Ensure that children have washed their hands before you begin.

2. Play gentle meditation music and invite children to sit or lie down comfortably.

3. Guide them through three deep belly breaths to start the activity.

4. Model how to spread out your three middle fingers on each hand to make a 'W'.

5. Invite the children to place the fingers on either side of their mouth and press down softly.

6. Encourage them to gently sweep their fingers across their faces with gentle pressure as if they were drawing cat's whiskers.

7. Model inhaling deeply as you run your fingers across your face and exhale as you lift your fingers at the end of the whiskers.

8. Repeat the sequence as many times as desired.

50 fantastic ideas for mindfulness

Mindful eating
Choosing positive and nurturing foods

What you need:

- A small piece of fruit, vegetable, biscuit or cracker per child

Top tip ⭐

Children will usually be more inclined to take part in this activity if you use familiar foods. Once they have tried the strategy a few times, expand to vegetables, savoury foods or new foods.

What's in it for the children?

This strategy allows children to become aware of the positive and nurturing foods we eat by engaging their senses.

Taking it forward

- Once the children have used the mindful eating strategy a few times, take it one step further by having children mindfully drink. This can be done with any liquid, including water.

✚ Health & Safety

Be aware of all food allergies and any cross contamination before undertaking this activity. Plan accordingly.

What to do:

1. Have the children look at the food they will be eating. Ask them what they notice about it. For example, what colour is it? Is it small or large?

2. Invite the children to smell the food. Does it have a smell? What does it smell like?

3. Have the children direct their attention to how it feels. Is it firm or soft? Can they squeeze it? Is it smooth, sticky or rough? Is it warm or cold?

4. Ask the children if the food makes any sounds.

5. Have the children very slowly put the piece of food in their mouth but not chew it! Challenge them to leave it on their tongue. How does it feel on the tongue? Can they taste anything yet? Does it smell different once it's in the mouth?

6. Have the children begin to chew slowly – one mindful chew at a time. Does the taste change? Ask them how it feels in the mouth.

7. Try to get them to notice when they swallow, and see how far they can feel the food move into their body.

8. Finally, discuss what they felt during the activity.

Mindful stepping stones

A focused breathing strategy for school and home

What you need:

- At least ten stepping stones, e.g. slices of logs, mats, balance stones

What to do:

1. Distribute the stepping stones equal distances from each other to make a path of any shape.

2. Explain to the children that this is a special kind of path and it helps us to be calm and happy.

3. Model what the children should do:

   a. Step on the first stone and take a deep belly breath.

   b. Hold the breath as you step to the next stone and then exhale the breath.

   c. Then, step on the third stone and take a deep belly breath. Hold the breath as you step on the fourth stone and then exhale.

   d. Keep repeating until you have finished the path.

Top tip ⭐

Remind the children that this isn't a race. They are to take their time and everyone behind them should be patient and wait for their turn.

What's in it for the children?

This activity forms the foundation for basic mindful walking that allows a person to be present and purposeful in the moment.

Taking it forward

- Instead of deep breathing on each step, add a photograph of an object or a colour that children can look for when they step on that stone. So, if the stone is red, they are to look for something around them that is red.

- Get the children to create their own path around the setting.

- Try mindful walking. Encourage children to practise taking smaller steps without the stepping stones. They should walk slowly, taking deep breaths with each step and looking at the ground so they can notice where they are stepping.

Mindful nature walks

Walking mindfully in nature brings us closer to it

What you need:

- A nature garden or wooded area

What to do:

1. Have the children stand still and take three deep belly breaths.

2. Remind them that their thoughts should remain on the walk and the beauty of nature around them.

3. Get the children to begin walking slowly, being aware of the heel-to-toe rhythm as their feet touch the ground.

4. Encourage them to focus their eyes softly forward as they walk.

5. Stop the children periodically and draw their attention to one natural object. Give them time to notice the detail, colour, how it feels and how it smells.

6. After everyone in the group has examined the natural object, talk them through another belly breath and continue walking.

7. Repeat this process for the length of time that is appropriate for your group.

8. Following the walk, have the children discuss what they saw on the walk and how it made them feel.

Top tip

Practise slow, mindful walking during a PE session so that the nature walk is about the mindfulness of the task.

What's in it for the children?

The slow, rhythmic movements of mindfully walking in nature help to relieve stress, calm the mind and body while also providing good exercise.

Taking it forward

- Give each child a small bag to collect the objects noticed along the walk. Following the walk, use the collected objects as a part of a nature study that they can sketch, paint or make as a collage. As part of an art display, the children could write about how they felt on their walk and how the objects made them feel.

38

Imagination yoga

What you need:

- A specific unit topic or theme
- Camera

What to do:

1. Identify the key vocabulary in your current topic that you want the children to learn and understand.

2. As you teach each new word, have the children explore how that word could be translated into a yoga-type pose. The pose will help them remember what the word means as that they attach meaning to a physical and mental state.

3. Agree as a group which pose best fits each word and ask everyone to make the same pose. Obvious poses might be on all fours for a polar bear (arctic theme) or with the arms pulled into the chest for a tyrannosaurus rex (dinosaur theme), but poses do not need to be so literal.

4. Take a photograph of the successful poses and make it into a poster with the vocabulary word under it. Add it to an area of provision.

5. Encourage the children to practise the poses while they are in that area or discussing the topic.

Top tip ⭐

In the beginning, children may not fully understand that you want them to be creative with their bodies. You may have to demonstrate several examples before they get the idea and begin to be creative with their poses.

What's in it for the children?

Children begin to reconnect with their bodies. This activity gives a variety of vocabulary hooks while also exercising the body. The poses will help children to remember the vocabulary.

Taking it forward

- Take the poses into your PE lessons as a warm up/cool down activity.

Mindful smiling

Smiles are contagious

What you need:

- Mirrors
- Camera
- Tokens
- Jar

....
Top tip ⭐

On average, children smile over 400 times a day and happy adults smile 40–50 times a day. Children tend to mirror what they see in their role models so make sure you keep smiling!
....

What's in it for the children?

It's been proven that smiling reduces stress. Smiling stimulates the brain's reward mechanisms, so it makes the smiler and the children who see the smile happier.

Taking it forward

- Using the photographs taken, crop out the smiles and create an activity where the children need to match the smiles to the children in the group.

What to do:

1. Ask the children, 'What is a smile?'. Take time to discuss their thoughts.

2. Invite the children to smile into a mirror and explore each other's smiles.

3. Use questions to prompt discussion, e.g. 'How does your face feel when you smile?', 'How does your body feel when you smile?', 'How do others look when they smile?'and 'How does the smiles of others make you feel?

4. Take a photograph of each child's smile and use these to make a display with positive quotes about smiles.

5. Set the children a smiling challenge. Every time they see someone else smiling, they should put a token in a smiling jar.

6. Set a smile target for the day. If the group meets the target, they get a small treat at the end of the day.

Follow me

A quiet game of *Simon Says*

What you need:

- Meditation music

Top tip ⭐

There is no right or wrong way to do the hand movements. Concentrate on the music and move to the music in a way that feels right to you.

What's in it for the children?

The focused attention and concentration required for this activity is relaxing and puts children in the present moment.

Taking it forward

- Use the strategy at the beginning or end of whole-school assemblies to allow children to begin their day on a positive note.

- Once the practice is established, have a child from the group lead the rest in the movements for others to follow.

What to do:

1. Begin with meditation music playing softly in the background.

2. Guide the group through a few deep belly breaths.

3. Explain to the children that they MUST pay attention and following the hand movements you make.

4. Model slow, deliberate hand movements that flow with the music being played.

5. Periodically, remind the children about what they are doing, why and how it helps them.

6. Have the children focus on the feeling of the movement of their hands, the breath through their noses and the calmness flowing through their bodies.

7. Finish the meditation with a few deep belly breaths.

Listening eggs

A mindful listening game

What you need:

- 12 plastic fillable eggs
- Six different small parts materials, e.g. rice, beans, beads, pennies
- Clear sticky tape
- An egg carton that holds at least 12 eggs

What to do:

1. Fill each egg with some of the small parts. Make two of each type of egg, e.g. two rice-filled eggs.

1. Secure the eggs using a small amount of sticky tape to keep them closed.

3. Place the eggs randomly into the carton.

4. Place the egg carton in a quiet place, e.g. the mindfulness corner (see p. 60)

5. Encourage the children to sit quietly and give an egg a shake, listening carefully to the sounds the material in the egg is making.

6. When they find two eggs with the similar sound, they can pair them up by placing them in the carton across from each other.

7. Encourage them to get another child to 'check' their work by also listening to the eggs and seeing if they agree that the sounds match.

Top tip ⭐

Don't get caught up in whether the child has got the matching eggs right or wrong. Be more focused on the concentration and effort the child in putting into identifying the matching sounds.

What's in it for the children?

This activity encourages conscious awareness of sounds and helps to improve listening skills.

Taking it forward

- Take photographs of the different materials and make small photo cards. Once the children have paired up the eggs, they can then match the photographs to the eggs based on the sound alone.

Mindful scents

What you need:

- Several small containers with secure lids, e.g. film canisters
- A screwdriver or craft knife
- A variety of scents that have calming or relaxing properties:
  - Cinnamon sticks
  - Nutmeg
  - Cloves
  - Frankincense oil
  - Peppermint oil
- Cotton balls
- Sticky tape
- Labels

What to do:

1. First, create the scent bottles for the children to use. Take several small lidded containers and make holes in the top of each lid using a screwdriver or craft knife. Fill each container with one of the scents you have chosen. If using the oils, sprinkle a few drops on a cotton ball and put that in a container. Seal the containers securely using sticky tape. Label each container.

2. Hide the containers in an accessible area of the provision and encourage children to use their sense of smell to find them.

3. Explain to the children that when they are in that area, they may like to take a scent bottle, put it close to their nose and take a deep belly breath with their eyes closed.

4. Encourage them to find their favourite scent.

5. Spend some time with the children in small groups so that they can discuss how the scents make them feel.

Top tip ⭐

Lavender may be an obvious scent to use. However, some children with ADD, ADHD or ASD may react badly to this scent.

What's in it for the children?

Children begin to recognise that scents can affect how they feel and they can use their favourite scents to calm down and relax.

Taking it forward

- Make two bottles of each scent and do not label one of them. Have the children try to match up the two scents through their sense of smell.

Mindful touch

Explore the sensations of a feely object

What you need:

- Any objects that encourage the use of touch to explore, e.g.
  - seashells
  - faux fur
  - slime
  - play dough
  - tree bark
  - fabric

What to do:

1. Invite a group of children to sit in a circle. Talk them through taking a few deep belly breaths before you begin.

2. Give each child a feely object. Ask them to let the object sit in their hands for a moment and notice the weight and the pressure it exerts.

3. Ask them to close their eyes and allow their hands to explore the object, running their fingers softly over any ridges and indentions. Really take the time to feel the object.

4. Encourage them to notice what they are feeling; relax into watching for as long as your concentration allows.

5. Invite them to mindfully touch every detail. Model using different body parts to explore the object, e.g. top of your hand, your cheeks, nose, arms.

6. Allow a few minutes to discuss what was noticed and how we can use this strategy to bring calm into our lives.

Top tip

Be aware that some people do not like some textures. Giving children a choice of objects will allow them to avoid those textures.

What's in it for the children?

Positive mindful touch is important for our wellbeing. Showing care for ourselves helps us show loving kindness to a very important person in our lives – ourselves. This strategy brings focus to children's sense of touch. It allows them the time to explore the sensations and feelings of an object as they take the time to mindfully touch it.

Taking it forward

- Take this strategy further by using in conjunction with mindful hand massage (see p. 33).

Calm down bottles

A visual reference to become calm and relaxed

What you need:

- One small drinks bottle per child
- Warm and cool water
- Glitter paint or glitter glue
- Biodegradeable glitter
- Sticky tape

What to do:

1. Fill a clean bottle three quarters full with warm (not hot) water.
2. Add approximately two tablespoons of glitter paint or glitter glue. The warm water helps to dilute the glue but the glue also thickens the water; allowing the glitter to stay suspended for a little longer.
3. Add another tablespoon of loose glitter.
4. Add cool water to fill the bottle and close tightly.
5. Seal the lid with sticky tape.
6. Give it a good shake and watch the glitter swirl around the bottle and slowly settle.
7. Invite the children to observe the calm down bottles. Shake the bottle and then set it down in front of the group.
8. As you watch the glitter swirling, encourage everyone to do deep belly breathes.
9. Talk about how we can allow ourselves to calm and settle as the glitter calms and settles.

Top tip ⭐

To ensure that the bottle stays closed, put a small drop of strong glue on the threads of the bottle and then tighten the cap.

What's in it for the children?

Explain to children that the swirling glitter is similar to what happens in our heads when we are upset, mad, angry, anxious, etc. The thoughts swirling about are all mixed up, moving quickly in and out of our mind. Breathing allows us to calm those thoughts, focusing our mind only on the glitter as it slows and settles, like our thoughts; then we can identify the emotions we are having and make the right choices on what to do next.

Taking it forward

- Encourage children to use this strategy at home and in the mindfulness corner (see p. 60) to self-regulate their emotions.

Mindful singing
Joyful mindful moments

What you need:

- A selection of songs that the children enjoy singing

Top tip ⭐

The key is to bring awareness to the moment of singing and bask in the joy of the sound without judgement.

What's in it for the children?

Singing is made up of deep inhales and long exhales which is natural calming strategy. We also know that music itself can have meditative properties. Thus, with just a little tweaking to your usual music routine, you can develop a mindful technique that can calm and relax children while also bringing enjoyment.

Taking it forward

- Have the children add instruments to their singing, bringing focus to the sounds of the instruments combined with the sounds of their voices. Encourage good deep breathing to enhance the enjoyment.

What to do:

1. Begin by having children sit up comfortably with their hands in their laps.

2. Have them take three deep belly breaths (see p. 6), bringing their attention to their breathing.

3. Start singing a familiar song and encourage the children to join in. Ask them to take nice, deep breaths while they are singing and focus on how the sound vibrates through their bodies as they sing.

4. After they finish singing the song, discuss how the singing made them feel. Ask questions such as, 'How does the sound feel in your mouth?', 'How does it make your tongue feel, or your throat or chest?', and 'How does singing make you feel emotionally?'.

Mindful slime

A sensory stimulus to calm and relax

What you need:

- Slime
- Tuff tray
- Camera

What to do:

1. Buy or make slime in advance of the activity (there are lots of great recipes online).

2. Prepare an area of provision for children to explore the properties of slime. Tuff trays work well for this.

3. Allow children to use the slime, encouraging them to focus on how it feels and what happens to it when they squeeze it, fold it, roll it, etc.

4. In small groups, facilitate a discussion on how playing with the slime makes them feel and how they can use it to calm themselves when they are mad, sad, angry or upset by letting it run through their fingers or by squeezing it tightly so that it squirts out between their fingers.

5. Photograph the children as they play with the slime. Use the photos to create activity cards showing ways to use the slime in a mindful way, e.g. squeeze, fold, roll.

Top tip ⭐

Keep some slime in your mindfulness corner so that children can have access to its calming features when they are in need.

What's in it for the children?

Deep pressure that happens when the children squeeze the slime sends signals to the brain that they are calm and this increases their focus. It also stimulates the brain to realise it is not in danger and allows the children to relax.

Taking it forward

- Consider adding scents, colour or textures to the slime depending on your children's preferences. Store the slime in airtight containers when not in use.

- If you make your own slime, glitter can be a great addition. However, there is a lot of concern around the environmental effect of glitter. There are some biodegradable glitters available that can be used that are just as pretty and less harsh on our environment.

Snake bag
Use pressure to ground and focus

What you need:

- Clean white tube sock
- Rice or dried beans
- Needle and thread
- Permanent markers

Top tip ⭐

Don't over-fill the sock. It needs to be loose so that it easily drapes while also adding pressure.

What's in it for the children?

The pressure provided by the snake bag helps children to feel grounded. This can promote a sense of wellbeing and enables them to focus on what is happening around them.

Taking it forward

- Use the snake bag as a heating pad. Microwave for one minute, check the temperature to ensure it is not too hot and then use as normal, or hold it in the hands or around the neck to promote greater relaxation and calmness.

What to do:

1. Make a snake bag by filling a long sock with rice or beans.

2. Double stitch the top of the sock to close it securely.

3. Invite the child decorate their snake using permanent markers.

4. Once it is ready explain to the children that the snake bag can help them to feel calm.

5. Model to the children how to lay the snake bag across the top portion of the lap near the hips when sitting down. Every child will be different and some may prefer to hold it in the centre of their lap or near their knees.

6. Store the snake bags in an accessible place in the provision. Encourage the children to collect their snake bag and use it whenever they need to be more focused, particularly when doing school work, listening to story or doing a meditation.

Thankful beanstalk

Emphasise gratitude in your setting

What you need:

- Brown display paper
- Wall space
- Staple gun or sticky tape
- Leaf template
- Colouring pencils

What to do:

1. Crush brown display paper to make a long beanstalk shape. This activity alone can be enjoyable for the children.

2. Make the beanstalk stem about a metre tall, starting from the floor with lots of twists and turns. Fix it to the wall with a staple gun or sticky tape.

3. Each week, invite each child to identify one thing they are thankful for. Explain that gratitude will help the beanstalk to grow.

4. Provide them with green leaf templates and ask them to create a leaf to go on the beanstalk.

5. As the stalk fills up, add more to the stem. Build excitement about the beanstalk growing one afternoon and then add another metre overnight.

What's in it for the children?

This activity helps children to develop a sense of gratitude as they regularly have to think of something they are thankful for. It supports the development of a positive attitude and gives them a sense of accomplishment because they are helping their beanstalk grow.

Taking it forward

- Challenge parents, carers, visitors and staff members to add their own leaves of thankfulness to the beanstalk each week and have them share their leaf with the group.

- Explore the topic of thankfulness and gratitude. At first children will tend to focus on physical items like a toy or a person. Encourage them to explore less tangible things to be thankful for like the sunshine, a blue sky, the rain, a smile, etc.

Worry pets
A safe place for small worries

What you need:

- Scissors
- Thick cardboard
- Coloured yarn
- Scraps of felt
- Glue

Top tip ⭐

Remind children that worry pets are for little worries. If they have a big worry, they should always tell an adult.

What's in it for the children?

A worry pet gives children the ability to manage their anxieties in a way that soothes them and allows them to get on with their day.

Taking it forward

- Discuss names for the worry pets and where they will live in the setting.

What to do:

1. First make a pom-pom maker. Cut a square out of thick cardboard. The larger the square, the larger the pom-pom it will make.

2. Cut a slit running down the middle to make it look like the letter U. Make several of these so that children can create their worry pets together in small groups.

3. Cut a short piece of yarn that will be used to tie off the pom-pom. Insert this piece into the slit you made.

4. Model how to wrap yarn around the pom-pom maker several times. The more wraps made, the fuller the pom-pom will be.

5. Find the ends of the short piece of yarn and tie it around the wrapped yarn with a tight knot.

6. Slide the yarn off the end of the U-shaped pom-pom maker. Turn it over, wrapping the yarn around, and tie an even tighter knot on the opposite side to the first knot.

7. Use scissors to cut the looped ends of the wrapped yarn. You have now created a pom-pom! It will come out looking very shaggy and a bit uneven. Trim to make it even if desired.

8. Cut small pieces of felt to make eyes and glue these to the pom-pom.

9. Encourage the children to access their worry pet for comfort and reassurance when they are feeling anxious, worried, upset or angry.

Feelings chart

What you need:

- A variety of emotions cards with a picture and the emotion word, e.g. a smiling face for 'happy'
- A photograph of each child

What to do:

1. Introduce a few of the basic emotions cards showing emotions that children will already be familiar with, e.g. happy, calm, sad, angry.

2. Each morning, when the child comes into the setting, ask them to decide on which emotion they are feeling at that moment and put that emotion card under their photograph with the support of an adult. (This could be used as part of your register.)

3. Spend a few minutes each day discussing some of the emotions the children are feeling and what things they can do to change some of the negative emotions.

4. As children develop an understanding of these emotions, begin adding a few new emotions such as annoyed, confused, shy, surprised, etc.

Top tip ⭐

Take it slowly and only introduce a few basic emotions at the start. It is important that we are getting the children to express their emotions first and then helping them to find ways to change the negative emotions.

What's in it for the children?

The children begin to develop a better understanding of their emotions and how they can do something to change them.

Taking it forward

- Encourage the children to change their emotions cards during the day as their emotions change or, for older children, when they have transition times such as after lunch.

Positive Post-it® day

Focus on both inner positivity and shared positivity

What you need:

- Lots of Post-it® notes in different colours, shapes and sizes
- Different coloured pens, pencils and markers

What to do:

1. Before the big day, let the children, parents, carers and staff know about Positive Post-it® day. Explain that the goal will be to plaster the room with things we are thankful for, compliments about others, things that make us happy or make us feel good.

2. Throughout the Positive Post-it® day, encourage everyone to write and/or draw anything that is positive on a Post-it® and stick their notes to the walls, shelves, doors, windows, etc.

3. At various points in the day, stop everything and read out or describe a few of the notes that are around the room.

4. Spend some time during the day discussing how it makes the children feel to write their notes or how it felt when they heard what was on them.

5. At the end of the day, encourage parents and carers to take some time to explore the notes around the room with their children.

What's in it for the children?

Children get a physical reminder of how being positive makes us feel good. They develop their social skills by identifying positive behaviours and traits in others.

Taking it forward

- Make a scrapbook of all the notes for children to look at after the day is over.

- Send some Post-it® notes home for children to do the activity with their families. Encourage families to take photos and share what they have done together.

- Encourage the rest of school and community to take part and use the hashtag #PositivePostItDay on social media to spread positivity outside your setting.

Fairy worry plaque

Fairy trees magically take away upset and worry

What you need:

- A log slice
- A marker pen
- A fairy bottle (calm down bottle, p. 46)

What to do:

1. Before the children come into the setting, create a worry plaque. In the centre of a log slice, draw around your hand with a marker. Around your hand print, write: 'A fairy's magic takes your worries away.'

2. Explain to the children that this is a special worry plaque made from a fairy tree. Introduce the fairy bottle and allow them to play with it for a while and speculate about it.

3. Explain that if they put their hand on the hand print and whisper their worry, the fairies magically trap the worry in the fairy bottle.

4. Invite one of the children to share a worry they have, then ask them to shake the fairy bottle and watch the fairy dust settle while taking deep belly breaths. Once the fairy dust has settled, the fairies will have taken away the worry.

5. If the worries come back, they can just go back and do it again.

Top tip ⭐

Remind children that the fairy worry plaque is for little worries. If they have a big worry, they should always tell an adult.

What's in it for the children?

This activity gives children control over their worries. The mindful focus on verbalising the worry in a whisper and using the fairy bottle (calm down bottle) allows them a moment to breathe deep and calm down.

Taking it forward

- Invite children to make their own fairy worry plaques and small fairy bottles to take home so that the whole family can have a bit of fairy magic.

Jar of kindness

A positive physical reminder of all the kindness happening around them

What you need:

- Strips of coloured paper
- Pen
- A clear jar or container labelled 'jar of kindness'
- Photographs, one of each child
- A simple poster with the words 'jar of kindness' on it

What to do:

1. Write the names of all the children and staff that work with them on individual coloured strips of paper. Fold these so the names cannot be seen.

2. Put the folded strips into the jar of kindness.

3. Create a jar of kindness poster with space to stick a photograph on it.

4. Begin each day by randomly drawing a name out of the jar. Stick this person's photograph onto the jar of kindness poster.

5. Discuss with the group what kind things they can do for that person today.

6. Over the course of the day, keep reminding everyone who the designated person is for the day and keep encouraging acts of kindness towards that person.

7. At the end of the day, take some time to ask how that person felt throughout the day and what acts of kindness they remember.

Top tip ⭐

In the beginning, you are going to have to use lots of visual and verbal cues to encourage the acts of kindness until it becomes a habit.

What's in it for the children?

Children will learn the importance of kindness and exactly what kindness is in everyday life. Focusing on being kind can change the mood and behaviour in the classroom.

Taking it forward

- After all people have had a chance to have a special day for themselves, start using the jar of kindness to mark acts of kindness as they happen. Add tokens, e.g. beads, to the jar for every kindness observed. Once the jar is filled, have a kindness celebration.

Acts of kindness challenge

Develop compassion and kindness into a habit

What you need:

- Kindness tokens e.g. marbles, coloured beads or pom-pom balls
- A small clear jar or container

What to do:

1. Discuss the idea of 'an act of kindness' with the children. Decide as a group what an act of kindness might look like, e.g. sharing toys or helping someone up who has fallen over.

2. Begin each week by either randomly choosing an act of kindness or pre-determine an act of kindness for the day. Share this with the group and model some of the things you will be looking for.

3. When an adult notices the act, they should put an act of kindness token in the jar.

4. At the end of each day, check your jar to see how close you are to the top.

5. When the jar of kindness is full, organise a little celebration for the group to enjoy.

Top tip ⭐

Make sure to highlight and celebrate acts of kindness several times during the day as you put tokens in the jar. This will act as a verbal and visual reminder.

What's in it for the children?

Once children are able to understand what an act of kindness is, they will start to see how kindness helps them to be happy as well as how it makes others happy. We are working towards kindness being a positive habit.

Taking it forward

- Share the act of kindness with parents and carers. Encourage them to participate as a family at home with their own jar and share their home celebrations with the group.

Loving kindness garden

Growing a garden using acts and thoughts of kindness

What you need:

- A large poster or display titled 'Loving kindness garden'
- Coloured display paper or fabrics
- Small flower templates of all shapes
- Crayons, pencil colours or felt tips

What to do:

1. Create a display or space in the setting to be your loving kindness garden. Set it up like a typical garden, using display paper to create grass, sky and sun.

2. Share with the children the loving kindness garden. Explain to them that their acts of kindness will make the garden grow and bloom.

3. When someone does or says something nice for them, children should colour in a little flower to add to the garden. They can also colour in a flower if they have done or said something nice to someone else.

4. Take photographs of the garden periodically as it grows to add to the display so they can see the changes as the acts of loving kindness make it grow.

5. End each day with this loving kindness mantra:

   May you be safe,
   May you be happy,
   May you be healthy,
   May you be peaceful.

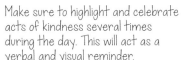

Top tip ⭐

Make sure to highlight and celebrate acts of kindness several times during the day. This will act as a verbal and visual reminder.

What's in it for the children?

Children learn to recognise kindness and exactly what it might look like in everyday life. In the beginning, the children will put lots of flowers in the garden, then it will decrease to a more manageable rate. If you mention the garden each day, it will soon become a habit.

Taking it forward

- Give an 'loving kindness award' each week to the child that showed the best or most loving kindness that week.

- Start a new garden with each new season or term.

Mindfulness corner

Children taking ownership of their mindfulness

What you need:

- A quiet area away from the busiest activities
- Comfortable seating and/or cushions
- Objects that promote mindfulness including calm down bottles (p. 46) and listening eggs (p. 34)

(p. 46) ... (p. 34)

Top tip ⭐

Share mindful objects and practise mindful activities before you add them to the mindfulness corner for independent use.

What to do:

1. Create a mindfulness corner to encourage children to manage their own mindfulness and emotions.

2. Make the mindfulness corner one that is based on pupil voice. Allow children to have input into what they would like to see in the corner that best supports their mindfulness development. This personalised space will give children ownership and lead to greater impact.

3. Take the time to consider the comfort of your children. The space should be one of tranquillity and peace.

4. Consider how to darken or mute the lightening in this space using fabrics, tents and sheltered areas.

5. Once the space is set up, agree ground rules with the children that fit the needs of your group.

What's in it for the children?

Providing a space that children can retreat to in times of stress validates the importance of mindful strategies. It provides a space for children to develop their emotional intelligence and self-regulate.

Taking it forward

- When the weather is nice, consider how you can make a mindful space outdoors that lends itself to allowing children to be present and grounded in nature. Encourage the children to create the spaces and use them.

- Choose a 'mindful child of the day' and allow that child to add a special object to the collection for the day. Encourage the child to tell their classmates why they added the object.

Mindful memories collage

A special 'vision board' that gives focus to happy memories

What you need:

- A large display titled 'mindful memories'
- A large sheet of paper
- Coloured pencils, felt tips or crayons

What to do:

1. Each week, as a group, discuss all of the good things about the week.
2. Agree on one thing that was good for the whole group. It can be as simple or big as the children want it to be; it can celebrate milestones of the group or an individual. The only criteria is that it has to be something that made everyone happy.
3. Ask each child to contribute a small drawing or object to the collage and arrange these on a large sheet of paper.
4. Date the collage and add a short caption, then add it to a mindful memories display.

Top tip ⭐

Encourage the children to share the mindful memories collage with their parents, carers and visitors as they come into the setting. Get them to verbalise the importance of all these memories and how the collage makes them feel.

What's in it for the children?

Children can have the tendency to focus on the negative things that happen around them and allow all the positive things to be easily forgotten. The mindful memories activity provides a reminder of all the good things that have happened with the children throughout the year.

Taking it forward

- Give each child their own mindful memories notebook and get them to draw and/or write what was the best thing that happened to them that day. It is a great way to bring positivity into the home and collect ideas for the weekly collage.

Calm down boxes

Individual personalised boxes to support wellbeing

What you need:

- Small boxes with lids
- Coloured pencils, felt tips or paint
- A variety of sensory objects that the child can choose from, e.g. glitter bottles, soft squeezy balls, hard spiky balls, stress balls, play dough, textured cloth, sea shells, small bean bags

What to do:

1. It is unlikely that you will need a calm down box for every child. This is a strategy to use for your most anxious children – those who have difficulty sharing mindful items and need extra special care and support.

2. Give the anxious child a small box and allow them time to decorate it as they choose.

3. Explain to the child that this is their own special box. This box will hold objects that make them feel good and calm.

4. Have a selection of objects for the child to explore. Ask questions about how the different objects feel, smell, look and how they make the child feel.

5. Invite them to choose five objects for their box that make them feel good.

6. Finally, choose a special place for them to keep their box.

7. Allow and encourage the child to use their special box when they are feeling overwhelmed, anxious, upset, sad, mad, etc.

Top tip ⭐

Over time, allow the child to add or change the objects in the box.

What's in it for the children?

Calm down boxes help to encourage children into a more peaceful state when they are anxious by occupying them with tangible, mindful objects.

Taking it forward

- As children handle the objects, encourage deep belly breathing to enhance the effects of the sensory objects. Refrain from talking to them until they are visibly more calm and ready to put the box away.

Mindful teacher
Develop your own mindfulness practice

What you need:
- Nothing

What's in it for the children?

The more mindful you become, the calmer you will be when dealing with the children. Your very words and actions will become more mindful and you will become a model for your children. Mindfulness will begin to become part and parcel of your pedagogy.

Taking it forward

- Take the plunge into really beginning to understand mindfulness and develop your practice. Here is a free eight-week Mindfulness-based stressed reduction programme can be done online in your own time and at your own pace: https://palousemindfulness.com/.

What to do:

Begin developing your own mindfulness with these four strategies:

1. **One-minute breathing meditation** – Close your eyes and take 15 deep belly breaths. Focus your attention on your nostrils. Notice the inhale and exhale of air, how it feels and how it makes your body feel.

2. **Mindful object meditation** – Choose an item you are wearing to be your mindful object. During the day, at any point you notice the item, touch it and take three deep mindful breaths.

3. **Be present** – During mundane tasks, e.g. making a cup of tea, focus solely on what is happening, what you are doing and what you are seeing, smelling, touching. Enjoy the moment noticing all the little things about the task you are doing.

4. **Gratitude diary** – At some point each day, take a minute or two to note something you have been grateful for during the day. It can be a big thing like you won the lottery or as small as the rainbow you saw on your way to work. Take a moment to bask in the happiness of those precious moments. Then, on days you are feeling down, flip through the pages and remind yourself of all the wonderful things that have happened to you.